The 5-Minute Mindfulness Journal

THE 5-MINUTE

mindfulness journal

Daily Practices for a Calmer, Happier You

Noah Rasheta

callisto
publishing
an imprint of Sourcebooks

Copyright © 2018 by Callisto Publishing LLC
Cover and internal design © 2018 by Callisto Publishing LLC
Illustration © AnnelyBlooms/Creative Market, cover, pp iii, x-xiii, 14-15, 18-21, 34-35; Alexandra Dzh/Shutterstock pp 8-9, 32-33, 58-63, 96, 110-111; Anastasiya Bleskina/ Shutterstock pp 54, 92-93; antalogiya/Shutterstock pp xiv, 26-27, 66-67, 82-83; Eisfrei/ Shutterstock pp xiv, 1, 10-13, 26-27, 66-67, 82-83, 94-95; Irtsya/Shutterstock pp 42, 80-81, 84-85, 98, 100-101, 105; kateka/Shutterstock p viii; Katya Bogina/Shutterstock pp 29, 65, 72-73; Magnia/Shutterstock pp 24-25, 50-53, 68-71; moopsi/Shutterstock pp 38-41, 90-91, 107, 120; Nikiparonak/Shutterstock pp v, 74-79, 119; ninanaina/Shutterstock pp 106-107, 116-117; PaperSphinx/Creative Market pp 44-45, 48-49, 88-89; suns07butterfly/ Shutterstock pp 3, 16, 22-23
Cover and Interior Designer: Merideth Harte
Editor: Melissa Valentine
Production Editor: Andrew Yackira

Published by Callisto Publishing LLC C/O Sourcebooks LLC
P.O. Box 4410, Naperville, Illinois 60567-4410
(630) 961-3900
callistopublishing.com

Printed and bound in Malaysia
OGP 2

This book belongs to:

_____

CONTENTS

"Right here is a good place to start. Start where you are."

—PEMA CHÖDRÖN

Introduction

MINDFULNESS: IT'S BEEN PRACTICED in ancient Eastern traditions for thousands of years and has recently gone mainstream in Western culture. But what is it? And how does one "practice" it?

Mindfulness has two layers: being in the present moment, and having a nonjudgmental awareness of being in the present moment. Imagine you are sitting outside looking up at the clouds. The act of observing the clouds is a form of being present. The nonjudgmental awareness would be recognizing that there's no such thing as a misshapen cloud. In other words, when you observe the clouds, you see them as they are, without imposing judgment like "this cloud is too fluffy," or "that cloud is too wispy." Practicing mindfulness means applying this same form of nonjudgmental observation to your thoughts, feelings, and emotions. Rather than labeling the clouds, or your thoughts, you just observe them floating by. This practice leads to a sense of peace and contentment as you learn to not get so tangled in the chaos that is often going on in the mind.

I'm here to tell you that five minutes of mindfulness a day is all it takes to start reaping its incredible benefits. As you develop your practice, remember that consistency is more important than duration. You'll experience more benefits if you consistently practice for five minutes every day than if you practice for several hours only once a week. That's why every exercise in this journal is designed to take five minutes or less.

I structured this book as a journal because writing can be a powerful way of bringing awareness to your thoughts and ideas. The act of writing forces you to slow down and take the time to translate your thoughts into words, and then let the thoughts go on the page. I designed this journal to be used from start to finish, 5 minutes at a time. Each exercise is a tool for building your mindfulness practice. Some exercises may seem simple, and some may require more effort. This is natural, and it varies from person to person. Sometimes, what worked well for you in the past won't work well in the future. This is because things are always changing and you are always evolving. The *you* who's reading this now is not the same you who will finish this journal and reread it down the line. Just go with the flow and try not to judge your experience too much. Let each exercise unfold as it will.

Mindfulness is a very personal practice. You'll feel the insight, wisdom, and peace on a deep level. But you're not the only one who will benefit from the practice. When you become a more mindful version of yourself, those around you will also be affected. For example, I practice mindfulness for myself in order to be more present for others in my life. My kids have a more mindful father, my wife has a more present and compassionate companion, and my employers and coworkers have a more conscious employee. The ripple effect of mindfulness is profound. After completing a few exercises in this book, you'll see what I mean!

One important thing to remember: Mindfulness is not just about feeling good (although it does make you feel good), it's about being good at feeling. While it's common to experience an increase of happiness, joy, and contentment while practicing mindfulness, it's also common to become more aware and present to other emotions you might be experiencing like anxiety, fear, or anger. This is okay. Let it all come and go. Mindfulness helps us become more skillful with handling our difficult emotions while at the same time making us more aware and present to the positive emotions. None of it is good or bad. It just is.

You Are Not Your Thoughts

The average person's heart will beat 80 times in a minute and their lungs will breathe 16 times in a minute. How many thoughts do you think you have in a minute? We don't generally think of ourselves as our heartbeat or our breath. So why do we tend to think that we are our thoughts?

The five-minute practices in this section will help you detach from your thoughts in order to cultivate a calmer mind.

"Don't believe everything you think. Thoughts are just that—thoughts."

—ALLAN LOKOS

What are you thinking about right now? Pause and observe some of your thoughts. Spend a few minutes writing down some of the thoughts that are popping into your mind. Observe the quality of your thoughts—are they rapid, slow, repetitive?

_____

_____

_____

_____

_____

_____

_____

_____

_____

_____

_____

_____

_____

_____

Do your thoughts follow a theme? If so, what's the theme right now? Think of a song . . . what song just popped into your head? Why do you think that specific song came to mind?

_____

_____

_____

_____

_____

_____

_____

_____

_____

_____

_____

_____

_____

_____

_____

Timing Your Thoughts

Set a timer for 60 seconds and check your pulse on your wrist or neck to see how many times your heart beats in 60 seconds. Next, count how many breaths you take in 60 seconds. Finally, reset the timer and for the next 60 seconds try to observe your thoughts. See if you can make a dot below for every thought that pops into your head during this time. Can you keep track? How many dots are there?

Turn Off the Autopilot

Sometimes we go through life in a habitual manner. We say, do, or think the same things over and over. Mindfulness can be a good way to break the cycle of habitual reactivity. Today, take five minutes to try something out of your ordinary routine. Brush your teeth with your left hand. Take a new route to work. Notice how it feels. What new thoughts arise as you break your routine?

Take a moment to ponder where your thoughts come from. Whether they're inherited from societal views, your family culture, or ideological beliefs, thoughts originate from somewhere. List some of the possible sources of your thoughts.

"The greatest weapon
against stress is our
ability to choose one
thought over another."

—WILLIAM JAMES

The 5-Minute Mindfulness Journal

How much control do you have over your thoughts?
Try to draw a circle without thinking of a circle. Think
only of a triangle or any other shape while drawing
the circle. But do not under any circumstances think
of a circle. Were you able to do it? Why or why not?

Notice how you are feeling right now. Label the emotion: hungry, angry, optimistic, eager, excited, and so on. Now try to notice your thoughts. Write a few down. Do your thoughts change based on how you're feeling? How many times a day might this happen?

Is there a thinker of your thoughts? Do you create your thoughts or do thoughts just happen and you perceive them? In the left column, write down some of the thoughts you are coming up with, and in the right column, write down some of the thoughts that seem to arise on their own. Which list was easier to write?

NATURALLY ARISING THOUGHTS	HABITUAL THOUGHTS

Notice the randomness of your thoughts. Some arise from past memories, others from present experiences, and some seem to come out of nowhere. What percentage of your thoughts would you say are totally random? How much attention do you tend to give to your random thoughts? Is it productive?

Your Inner Narrator

Right now, there's a voice in your head. It's probably reading these words to you. Can you hear it? That narrator is always making meaning of things. I bet it's deciding if it agrees or disagrees with this book so far. It could even be saying, "What voice in my head? I don't have a voice in my head." That's the one! That's your inner narrator! The five-minute prompts that follow will help you become more aware of this voice and the stories it tells you.

"Wherever you go,
there you are."

—JON KABAT-ZINN

Wherever you go, your narrator is there too. What does your narrator sound like? Does it happen to sound like you? Does it like to repeat itself? Write down some of the common expressions you hear this voice saying inside your head.

Our inner narrator is skilled at coming up with elaborate stories about things. If a car cuts us off, the narrator convinces us that a jerk is behind the wheel. Are you upset at anyone today? Perhaps a coworker, friend, family member, or stranger? If so, what's the story the inner narrator is telling you? Write it down below.

Don't believe
everything you think.
Thoughts are just
that—thoughts.

—ALLAN LOKOS

Now, reread your story. What parts do you know for certain to be true? Identify the facts and then examine the rest—where did it come from? Could parts of your story be based on assumption rather than reality? Have you ever been around someone who tells the same story over and over, and maybe doesn't realize it? Your inner narrator is like that. There may be stories you have about yourself or others that you tell yourself over and over without even realizing it or stopping to consider if it's still true. What are some of the stories that your inner narrator continually repeats?

Have you ever had a story in your mind about something someone did or said, only to find out later that you were wrong about the story? Write both versions below.

What I thought was happening was . . .

_____

_____

_____

_____

_____

What was really happening was . . .

_____

_____

_____

_____

_____

Stories versus Reality

We tend to think that the voice of the narrator (aka: our thoughts) is omniscient. It's always right. It knows what others are thinking about us. It generates fears about things that haven't happened yet. It judges. It has lots of opinions. And it never stops talking. Today, pay attention to the voice. Recognize that the voice may be wrong! Just observe and see how that feels. You may notice yourself becoming less reactive.

What are you NOT thinking or worrying about right now? Consider the fact that right now, you may be experiencing the joy of not having a toothache. Had you thought about that? Write down some of the other joyful experiences you are having right now that were not in your immediate sphere of awareness. How does it feel to shift your focus like this?

"Meditation is not evasion; it is a serene encounter with reality."

—THÍCH NHẤT HẠNH

Befriending Your Inner Narrator

Let's be honest, if you're like most people, your inner narrator is kind of mean to you. "You idiot! Why did you do that? You look horrible today!" I'm sure you've heard some of these—and probably worse—expressions come from your own mind. If we spoke to others the way many of us speak to ourselves, we wouldn't have very many friends. Since it can be so harsh and cruel, you probably aren't a huge fan of your inner narrator. But what would happen if you befriended the voice in your head? The point of the exercises in this section is to better understand your own mind. Because the more you understand yourself, the easier it becomes to befriend yourself.

"Meditation practice isn't about trying to throw ourselves away and become something better. It's about befriending who we are already."

—PEMA CHÖDRÖN

In your head, are you the one who's listening or the one who's talking? Which voice is really you? Pause for a moment and try to identify the voice of the inner narrator. Write down how it feels when you're listening to yourself. Now, compare that to how it feels when you are the one talking to yourself. Which do you do more of?

What is the meanest thing you've ever said to someone? How do you feel about it? What is the meanest thing you've said (or say) to YOURSELF? Write about the experiences here, and compare how you tend to treat yourself versus how you treat others:

What Would You Say to Your Inner Narrator?

Imagine you're about to meet the voice that's been in your head for all these years. It looks like you, and sounds like you, but it's not you. List five compliments (what does the voice do for you?) and five complaints you have about the voice.

COMPLIMENTS

COMPLAINTS

_____   _____

_____   _____

_____   _____

_____   _____

_____   _____

_____   _____

Be Nice to Yourself

Say a nice thing about yourself now. Write it
here and then read it aloud:

How did that feel? Does your inner narrator have anything to say about what you just did? If your inner narrator responded with something critical, try closing your eyes and tuning in to the kind thing you just said until the narrator quiets down. How does that feel?

"The better you know
yourself, the better
your relationship with
the rest of the world."

—TONI COLLETTE

What makes you *you*? If someone were to say, "Tell me
a bit about yourself," how would you answer? Think of
some things that make you *you* and list them below.

I am:

_____

_____

_____

_____

_____

_____

_____

_____

Are any of the items on this list permanent traits or
attributes? Are any of these recent developments?
Circle the one that is most recent. The inner narrator
is always telling us a story about ourselves, often a
fictional one. When we see the impermanent nature
of our traits, we can see the impermanent nature of
the story, too.

Who will you be in the future? If someone five years from now were to say, "Tell me a bit about yourself," how would you answer?

Future you would say, I am:

_____

_____

_____

_____

_____

What story are you telling yourself about where you are now versus where you want to be in the future? What are you waiting for, really? What steps can you take today to start working toward the person you want to be?

_____

_____

_____

_____

_____

"Basically, you're not alone in there. There are two distinct aspects of your inner being. The first is you, the awareness, the witness, the center of your willful intention; and the other is that which you watch. The problem is, the part that you watch never shuts up."

—MICHAEL SINGER

What are you good at? In the left column, write down a few things that you're good at or some of the unique skills and qualities you have.

If your narrator has a negative response to any of these qualities, write the response in the right column.

_____	_____
_____	_____
_____	_____
_____	_____
_____	_____
_____	_____
_____	_____

Notice if the inner narrator wants you to doubt the positive things you have to say about yourself. Take a moment to hear what the inner narrator has to say. You can acknowledge the responses, but that doesn't mean your inner narrator is right! As you get in the habit of noticing the narrator's responses, you'll be able to let them go without attaching to them.

Do Others Have an Inner Narrator Too?

Think about someone you know, someone you like. What do you think their inner narrator says to them? Knowing this person, what do you want to say to their inner narrator? Write a letter to this person to "break the news" that there is an inner narrator doing a lot of talking, and that they don't need to believe everything they hear. Tell this person why they matter to you.

Dear   ,

....

....

....

....

....

With love,

Finding Peace in the Struggle

The peace of mind we gain through mindfulness arises in spite of the presence of difficult emotions. In other words, we don't gain peace of mind by eradicating stressful emotions like anger or sadness; we gain it by accepting and ultimately becoming more comfortable with these emotions. Instead of resisting painful thoughts, feelings, and experiences, we invite them in. We learn to sit with all types of emotions without labeling any as "good" or "bad."

"When we protect ourselves so we won't feel pain, that protection becomes like armor, like armor that imprisons the softness of the heart."

—PEMA CHÖDRÖN

What difficult event have you experienced in your life? Think of a time in your past when things felt like they were falling apart. As you reflect, notice if anything beautiful or powerful eventually arose from that experience. Write about what came from that experience, and how it changed you.

What are some difficult things in your life right now?
Write them down below.

Take a deep breath and think about where these challenges could lead you. As you think about your current challenges with a wider perspective, consider what lessons they may have in store. Look at the list you just wrote and try to imagine what possible good could come from these difficulties. Make a list below.

_____

_____

_____

_____

_____

_____

_____

_____

Reflect on what you wrote. Are you able to see your difficulties in a new light? Over the next few days, try to accept these challenges for what they are, rather than push them away.

Zooming Out to the Bigger Picture

When difficulties arise, we have the tendency to zoom in and only see the situation from our own perspective. Try zooming out to see the bigger picture. For example, a flat tire is inconvenient for you, but what about the tire shop employee? For them, it's good news. Try to practice seeing the bigger picture today and see how it feels.

"You can't stop the waves, but you can learn to surf."

—JON KABAT-ZINN

What is your greatest fear? Why do you think you have this fear? Where did it come from?

_____

_____

_____

_____

_____

_____

_____

_____

_____

_____

_____

_____

_____

Now, imagine if you weren't afraid of the thing you
fear. How would your life be different? How would
you feel?

Welcoming All Thoughts and Emotions

Picture your mind as a house. Inside the house there is a table. Your mind is the host and your thoughts and emotions are the guests. Around the table below, label all the guests you anticipate arriving. Draw a smiley face next to the guests you're happy to see and a frown next to those you wish had stayed home. It's natural to feel aversion toward some emotions and desire others to linger longer. What would it feel like to drop the animosity you have toward your uncomfortable emotions? What if you welcomed them all to the table?

Which emotions feel the most unpleasant to you?
Which emotional states do you tend to push away or
avoid? How much energy and time go into the effort
to avoid such emotions?

What is something you are really worried about right now? When we understand our aversions, we can develop a more mindful relationship with the fear and worry. Write down a list of some things you are worried about right now in your life. Why do these things worry you?

What is something you are excited about right now?
Likewise, when we understand what we desire and why
we desire it, we can approach our desires in a more
skillful way. We bring perspective to both excitement
and worry, without valuing one over the other. Write
down a list of some of the things you are most excited
about. Why are you so excited about these things?

"I've had a lot of
worries in my life,
most of which
never happened."

—MARK TWAIN

Greetings, Feelings

No matter what emotion you encounter today, try to offer it a warm greeting. You can visualize yourself saying something like "Oh, hello, anger! It's you again. Come give me a big hug!" Instead of pushing away the uncomfortable thoughts and emotions that arise throughout your day, see what happens when you start to welcome them, just as you would happiness or joy.

Love or Fear?

Most, if not all, of our emotional states stem from one of two places: a place of love or a place of fear. Consider your current emotional state. Can you trace it to one of these two root emotions? Write about this below. Whenever you feel a strong or difficult emotion, pause to consider its root. In doing so, you bring more perspective and understanding to your fleeting emotions.

What do you dislike about yourself? Write down five things that come to mind. Now consider if fear could be the root of any of these dislikes. What are you afraid of, and how does that lead to these qualities or characteristics? Write the corresponding fear in the right-hand column.

DISLIKE	ROOT FEAR

What do you like about yourself? Write down five things you like about yourself. Is love at the root of any of those likes? Draw a heart next to any that feel rooted in love.

_____

_____

_____

_____

_____

_____

_____

_____

_____

_____

_____

_____

_____

Label Your Emotions

When you're experiencing an emotion, rather than getting swept away in it, notice it for what it is and label it. Instead of thinking "I am angry," tell yourself "I am experiencing anger right now." Notice how you feel when you stay with the experience while not getting attached to it. Try labeling a few emotions below.

Self-Acceptance

When we look at the clouds in the sky, we accept them just as they are. In order to befriend your own mind, you must learn to accept yourself. Rather than try to change your feelings, thoughts, experiences, short-comings, fears, and struggles, accept them in this moment. Change is inevitable anyway. You don't need to change or improve before you can love yourself. Self-love is possible in this moment, just as you are. The following prompts are designed to help you understand this.

"Much of spiritual life is self-acceptance, maybe all of it."

—JACK KORNFIELD

What are some things that you believe to be your flaws? Include criticisms that others have made of you. Don't judge whether these things are accurate or "true," simply make a list. Notice if any discomfort arises as you think of these things and write them down. Stay present with the discomfort.

Look through the list of traits and ask yourself, "Is this an accurate assessment?" If some things are only accurate under certain circumstances, explore those circumstances below. If some things were accurate in the past, but are no longer accurate, write about those as well. If some things are indeed accurate, sit with them. How do you feel? Can you love yourself even with these shortcomings?

Flip the Script

As you examine your unfavorable traits, consider if there are positive aspects to them. For example, let's say I realize that I can be blunt and at times mean. In exploring this trait, I also recognize that I am willing to stand up for myself (and others) with honest and direct communication. In looking at the positive aspects of my traits, I begin to have more self-compassion.

The next time you make a mistake, or say or do something that you regret, picture a friend or a loved one doing the same. What would you say to them? Write it out below, but address the words to yourself.

"There is something wonderfully bold and liberating about saying yes to our entire imperfect and messy life."

—TARA BRACH

What makes a great friend? Think of some of the closest or best friends you've had. What made them such great friends? Write down some of the qualities and attributes that separate a friend from a great friend.

How would your life be different if YOU were a better friend to yourself? Write down five things you can do starting right now to be a better friend to yourself.

Write a brief letter to your 12-year-old self. First, tell younger you why you think you're awesome and why you're proud of yourself. Then explain what you've learned since then, including your biggest accomplishments and regrets. What advice would you give to the younger you?

_____

_____

_____

_____

_____

_____

_____

_____

_____

_____

_____

_____

Now, imagine you just received a letter from an older you, 10 years from now. What would that older you say to the present you? Why do they think you're awesome and why are they proud of you? What do you still have to learn? Write a letter from the viewpoint of having 10 more years of experience and perspective.

Accept Things as They Are

Practice accepting things right now (that doesn't mean you have to like them). Keep in mind, acceptance is not the same as resignation. It's about working with reality and not against it. Throughout the day, remind yourself: This is how things are. I accept this reality. How can I skillfully work within this reality?

Gratitude

We search far and wide for happiness. We work hard and save money thinking we can secure it, we spend our whole lives chasing it, and we hire teachers and coaches trying to enhance it. But at the end of the day, happiness remains elusive for many. The truth is that the moment we want to be happier is the moment we are no longer happy. Real joy exists in the present. Cultivating gratitude for the things we already have is the path to contentment.

"Look closely and you will find that people are happy because they are grateful."

—DAVID STEINDL-RAST

What are you grateful for right now? Make a list.
Avoid listing too many possessions, try to think about
experiences, relationships, moments, beauty, and the
things in life that are not just "stuff."

I'm grateful for . . .

Make a list of instances where you recall feeling a lot of joy or happiness. What was happening around you? What was happening inside you?

_____

_____

_____

_____

_____

_____

_____

_____

_____

Can you see a correlation between your happiness and gratitude? Look at the list of instances you just made. Put a star next to any that stem from a sense of gratitude for a person, place, situation, or opportunity.

Create a Gratitude Trigger

This trigger will serve as a prompt to pause and ask: "What am I grateful for right now?" For example, let's say a red traffic light is your gratitude trigger. Every time you hit a red light, it can be your moment to pause and think about what you are grateful for. This simple practice will help you find gratitude every single day.

"The little things? The little moments? They aren't little."

—JON KABAT-ZINN

Now, recall some events from your past where you felt happiness or joy. You can go as far back as childhood. List 5 to 10 events below.

_____

_____

_____

_____

_____

_____

_____

_____

Look at the list you just made and see if you can spot a common thread between these events. Do they involve family, friends, travel, relaxation, a new challenge, or something else? Circle the items on the list that have a common theme.

Once you know these themes, you can cultivate more gratitude for these types of moments and events throughout your life.

What's a "Good" Day?

We tend to project what is "good" or "bad" about any given situation based on our own unique experience. What's more, humans tend to have a negativity bias, so it can be easier to focus on what went "wrong" than what went "right." Take a few minutes to list some things that aren't quite going the way you want them to right now. Then, in the second list, write down some things that are going well right now. Which list was easier to write? Are both lists accurate?

What's a "Bad" Day?

Look at the list of the "good" things you have going on. See if you can find another perspective for any of these situations. Is it possible that someone else would think they were "bad"? For example: You landed a new deal or client at work—that's great! But somewhere a competitor is disappointed that they didn't land the deal, and maybe they are having a bad day. See—nothing is ever good or bad; it's just our perspective that makes it so.

You can't force yourself to be happy. Instead, allow happiness to arise naturally by reflecting on what you're grateful for. If you're having trouble thinking of something you're grateful for—if you're having a really hard time and can't shake the negative thoughts— focus on one important person, relationship, or situation in your life right now. Close your eyes and focus on that one thing. Consider what brought this person, relationship, or situation into your life—all the things that had to happen for this to be how it is right now. How do you feel? Write down what comes to mind.

Peace as the End Goal

We often find ourselves saying or doing things because we think they will make us happy. What if happiness wasn't the goal? What if it was peace? Think about the things you say, think, and do often for instant gratification. What if inner peace was the goal instead? Would you still be doing the same things? What would you do differently?

Cultivating Loving-kindness

Loving-kindness is a sense of consideration and tenderness toward others—and yourself. When you understand and love yourself, it becomes easy and natural to love and accept others as they are (not how you want them to be!). This comes down to the classic analogy of the airline safety protocol: Always place the oxygen mask on yourself first and then help those around you. Mindfulness is a ripple effect with endless possibilities. The five-minute prompts in this section will help you develop loving-kindness.

"You yourself, as much as anybody in the entire universe, deserve your love and affection."

—UNKNOWN

What do you love about yourself? List some of the qualities or attributes that you love about yourself below. How do these attributes benefit you? How do these attributes benefit others, especially the people you love?

What do others love about you? You may need to ask for some help with this one. Ask a family member or friend to list some of the qualities or attributes that they love most about you. Compare this list to the one you wrote about yourself—what are the similarities? Differences? Do you struggle to see in yourself what others see in you?

If you could magically give yourself any gift today, what would it be? Why did you choose that gift? How would that gift make your life different? Why do you feel you deserve that gift?

Loving-kindness Meditation

Repeat the following mantra:

May I be happy
May I be at peace
May I be free from suffering

Notice how it feels to wish this for yourself.

Now think of someone you love,
and express this same wish for them:

May you be happy
May you be at peace
May you be free from suffering

Notice how this feels.

"Be kind whenever possible. It is always possible."

—DALAI LAMA

How do you treat someone you love?

Think of someone you love deeply. Love and kind-ness toward this person looks like this:

DOS   DON'TS

How should you treat yourself?
  When you have love and kindness toward yourself
you should . . .

DOS	DON'TS

Reflect on the preceding lists. Do you regularly practice these dos and don'ts? Could you more mindfully
remember to do or not do these things throughout
your day?

"If you want others to be happy, practice compassion. If you want to be happy, practice compassion."

—DALAI LAMA

Starting Today

Make a resolution to be more kind and loving to yourself. Make a list of the things you are going to start or stop doing and saying today in order to treat yourself better.

STARTING TODAY,
I'M GOING
TO START . . .

STARTING TODAY,
I'M GOING
TO STOP . . .

What does compassion mean to you? How would you define it in your own words? Does everyone deserve it or does it need to be earned?

Think of a time when you've felt compassion for someone. Who was it and what were they going through? Write down a brief summary. Was the feeling of compassion natural? Where did it come from? How did it make you feel?

Compassion for Everyone

Try to see compassion as a sensitivity to the suffering that others experience, along with the desire to alleviate that suffering. Compassion doesn't need to be earned. Spend some time thinking about your circle of friends and family. Have you been holding back your compassion for anyone? Have you been caught up in whether a person "deserves" it or not? What if you let that go, and instead allowed compassion to flow freely? What would happen?

"If your compassion
does not include yourself,
it is incomplete."

—JACK KORNFIELD

Now that you've worked your way through this journal, reflect on how mindfulness affects your life.

Mindfulness makes my days . . .

_____
_____
_____
_____
_____
_____

I want to be more mindful because . . .

_____
_____
_____
_____
_____
_____

With more mindfulness, my life can be . . .

_____

_____

_____

_____

_____

_____

_____

Mindfulness changes my relationships with others
because . . .

_____

_____

_____

_____

_____

_____

_____

Start Over Again and Again and Again

Life is a continual process of becoming. Every moment that passes gives rise to a new moment in which you get to be present all over again. You're under no obligation to be the person you were in the past. From this moment on, give yourself the freedom to start fresh over and over and over again.

Further Reading for Your Mindfulness Journey

Mindfulness is a way of life. Your journey has just begun. If you would like to learn more about mindfulness and continue your practice, below is a list of books I recommend to help guide you along your journey.

Self-Compassion: The Proven Power of Being Kind to Yourself, by Dr. Kristin Neff

The Gifts of Imperfection: Let Go of Who You Think You're Supposed to Be and Embrace Who You Are by Brené Brown

Loving-kindness: The Revolutionary Art of Happiness, by Sharon Salzberg

Radical Acceptance: Embracing Your Life with the Heart of a Buddha, by Tara Brach

Daring Greatly: How the Courage to Be Vulnerable Transforms the Way We Live, Love, Parent, and Lead, by Brené Brown

The Happiness Trap: How to Stop Struggling and Start Living: A Guide to ACT, by Russ Harris

The Miracle of Mindfulness, Gift Edition: An Introduction to the Practice of Meditation, by Thích Nhất Hạnh

About the Author

NOAH RASHETA is a Buddhist teacher, lay minister, and author, as well as the host of the podcast *Secular Buddhism*. He teaches mindfulness and Buddhist philosophy online and in workshops all around the world. He works with others to make the world a better place as he studies, embodies, and teaches the fundamentals of Buddhist philosophy, integrating Buddhist teachings with modern science, humanism, and humor. He lives in Kamas, Utah, with his wife and three kids.